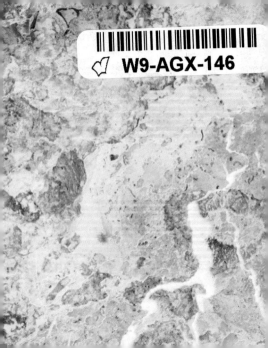

This book belongs to

_____

A Little Sip of Chicken Soup for the Soul®

*Inspiring Stories
of Self-Affirmation*

**Andrews McMeel
Publishing**

Kansas City

ISBN: 0-8362-5087-7

A Little Sip of Chicken Soup for the Soul®

*Inspiring Stories
of Self-Affirmation*

Inspired by the #1 *New York Times* bestseller

by Jack Canfield and Mark Victor Hansen

The Little Boy

by Helen E. Buckley

A Little Sip of Chicken Soup for the Soul®

*Inspiring Stories
of Self-Affirmation*

Inspired by the #1 *New York Times* bestseller

by Jack Canfield and Mark Victor Hansen

The Little Boy

by Helen E. Buckley

Once a little boy went to school.
He was quite a little boy.
And it was quite a big school.
But when the little boy
Found that he could go to his room
By walking right in from the
　　door outside,
He was happy.
And the school did not seem
Quite so big any more.

One morning,
When the little boy had been in
    school a while,
The teacher said:

"Today we are going to make
    a picture."
"Good!" thought the little boy.
He liked to make pictures.
He could make all kinds:
Lions and tigers,
Chickens and cows,
Trains and boats –
And he took out his box of crayons
And began to draw.

But the teacher said:
"Wait! It is not time to begin!"
And she waited until everyone looked
    ready.

"Now," said the teacher,
"We are going to make flowers."
"Good!" thought the little boy,
He liked to make flowers,
And he began to make beautiful ones
With his pink and orange and blue crayons.

But the teacher said,
"Wait! And I will show you how."
And she drew a flower on the blackboard.
It was red, with a green stem.
"There," said the teacher.
"Now you may begin."

The little boy looked at the teacher's flower.
Then he looked at his own flower,
He liked his flower better than the teacher's.
But he did not say this,

He just turned his paper over
And made a flower like the teacher's.
It was red, with a green stem.

On another day,
When the little boy had opened
The door from the outside all
    by himself,
The teacher said,
"Today we are going to make some-
    thing with clay."
"Good!" thought the little boy.
He liked clay.

He could make all kinds of things
    with clay:
Snakes and snowmen,
Elephants and mice,
Cars and trucks –

And he began to pull and pinch
His ball of clay.

But the teacher said,
"Wait! It is not time to begin!"
And she waited until everyone looked ready.

"Now," said the teacher,
"We are going to make a dish."
"Good!" thought the little boy,
He liked to make dishes,
And he began to make some
That were all shapes and sizes.

But the teacher said,
"Wait! And I will show you how."
And she showed everyone how to make
One deep dish.
"There," said the teacher,
"Now you may begin."

The little boy looked at the
        teacher's dish
Then he looked at his own.
He liked his dishes better than the
        teacher's
But he did not say this,
He just rolled his clay into a big
        ball again,
And made a dish like the teacher's.
It was a deep dish.

And pretty soon
The little boy learned to wait
And to watch,
And to make things just like the
        teacher.
And pretty soon
He didn't make things of his
        own anymore.

Then it happened
That the little boy and his family
Moved to another house,
In another city,
And the little boy
Had to go to another school.

This school was even Bigger
Than the other one,
And there was no door from the outside
Into his room.
He had to go up some big steps,
And walk down a long hall
To get to his room.

And the very first day
He was there, the teacher said,
"Today we are going to make a picture."

"Good!" thought the little boy,
And he waited for the teacher
To tell him what to do
But the teacher didn't say anything.
She just walked around the room.

When she came to the little boy,
She said, "Don't you want to make
      a picture?"
"Yes," said the little boy.
"What are we going to make?"
"I don't know until you make it," said
      the teacher.
"How shall I make it?" asked the
      little boy.
"Why, any way you like," said the
      teacher.
"And any color?" asked the little boy.
"Any color," said the teacher,

"If everyone made the same picture,
And used the same colors,
How would I know who made what,
And which was which?"
"I don't know," said the little boy.
And he began to make pink and orange
and blue flowers.

He liked his new school,
Even if it didn't have a door
Right in from the outside!

Risking

by Patty Hansen

Two seeds lay side by side in the fertile spring soil.

The first seed said, "I want to grow! I want to send my roots deep into the soil beneath me and thrust my sprouts through the earth's crust above me. ... I want to unfurl my tender buds like banners to announce the arrival of spring. ... I want to feel the warmth of the sun on my face and the blessing of the morning dew on my petals!"

And so she grew.

The second seed said, "I am afraid. If I send my roots into the ground below, I don't know what I will encounter in the dark. If I push my way through the hard soil above me, I may damage my delicate sprouts. ...What if I let my buds open and a snail tries to eat them? And if I were to open my blossoms, a small child may pull me from the ground. No, it is much better for me to wait until it is safe."

And so she waited.

A yard hen scratching around in the early
spring ground for food found the waiting
seed and promptly ate it.

MORAL OF THE STORY

Those of us who refuse to risk and grow get
swallowed up by life.

Discouraged?

by Jack Canfield

As I was driving home from work one day, I stopped to watch a local Little League baseball game that was being played in a park near my home. As I sat down behind the bench on the first-baseline, I asked one of the boys what the score was.

"We're behind 14 to nothing," he answered with a smile.

"Really," I said. "I have to say you don't look very discouraged."

"Discouraged?" the boy asked with a puzzled look on his face. "Why should we be discouraged? We haven't been up to bat yet."

Millie's Mother's Red Dress

by Carol Lynn Pearson

t hung there in the closet
While she was dying, Mother's
        red dress,
Like a gash in the row
Of dark, old clothes
She had worn away her life in.

    They had called me home
And I knew when I saw her
She wasn't going to last.

When I saw the dress, I said
"Why, Mother – how beautiful!
I've never seen it on you."

"I've never worn it," she slowly said.
"Sit down, Millie – I'd like to undo
A lesson or two before I go, if I can."

23

I sat by her bed
And she sighed a bigger breath
Than I thought she could hold.
"Now that I'll soon be gone,
I can see some things.
Oh, I taught you good – but I taught
   you wrong."

"What do you mean, Mother?"
"Well – I always thought
That a good woman never takes
   her turn,
That she's just for doing for
   somebody else.
Do here, do there, always keep
Everybody else's wants tended and
   make sure
Yours are at the bottom of the heap.

"Maybe someday you'll get to them.
But of course you never do.
My life was like that – doing for your dad,
Doing for the boys, for your sisters, for you."

"You did – everything a mother could."

"Oh, Millie, Millie, it was no good –
For you – for him. Don't you see?
I did you the worst of wrongs.
I asked for nothing – for me!

"Your father in the other room,
All stirred up and staring at the walls –
When the doctor told him, he took
It bad – came to my bed and all but shook
The life right out of me. 'You can't die,
Do you hear? What'll become of me?
What'll become of me?'

It'll be hard, all right, when I go.
He can't even find the frying pan,
   you know.

"And you children –
I was a free ride for everybody,
   everywhere.
I was the first one up and the last
   one down
Seven days out of the week.
I always took the toast that got
   burned.
And the very smallest piece of pie.

"I look at how some of your brothers
Treat their wives now
And it makes me sick, 'cause it
   was me
That taught it to them. And they
   learned.

They learned that a woman doesn't
Even exist except to give.
Why, every single penny that I could save
Went for your clothes, or your books,
Even when it wasn't necessary.
Can't even remember once when I took
Myself downtown to buy something
    beautiful –
For me.

"Except last year when I got that red dress.
I found I had 20 dollars
That wasn't especially spoke for.
I was on my way to pay it extra on
    the washer.
But somehow – I came home with this
    big box.
Your father really gave it to me then.

'Where you going to wear a thing
        like that to –
Some opera or something?'
And he was right, I guess.
I've never, except in the store,
Put on that dress.

"Oh Millie – I always thought if
        you take
Nothing for yourself in this world
You'd have it all in the next somehow.
I don't believe that anymore.
I think the Lord wants us to have
        something –
Here – and now.

"And I'm telling you, Millie, if some
        miracle
Could get me off this bed, you
        could look

For a different mother, 'cause I would be one.
Oh, I passed up my turn so long
I would hardly know how to take it.
But I'd learn, Millie.
I would learn!"

It hung there in the closet
While she was dying, Mother's red dress,
Like a gash in the row
Of dark, old clothes
She had worn away her life in.

Her last words to me were these:
"Do me the honor, Millie,
Of not following in my footsteps.
Promise me that."

I promised.
She caught her breath
Then Mother took her turn
In death.

We know everything we need to know to end the needless emotional suffering that many people currently experience. High self-esteem and personal effectiveness are available to anyone willing to take the time to pursue them.

Love Is Stronger ...

by John Wayne Schlatter

Having a goal based on love is the greatest life insurance in the world.

If you had asked my dad why he got up in the morning, you would have found his answer disarmingly simple: "To make my wife happy."

Mom and Dad met when they were nine. Every day before school, they met on a park bench with their homework. Mom corrected Dad's English, and he did the same with her math.

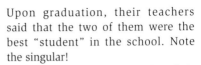

Upon graduation, their teachers said that the two of them were the best "student" in the school. Note the singular!

They took their time building their relationship, even though Dad always knew she was the girl for him. Their first kiss occurred when they were 17, and their romance continued to grow into their 80s.

Just how much power their relationship created was brought to light in 1964. The doctor told Dad he had cancer and estimated that he had six months to one year left at the most.

"Sorry to disagree with you, Doc," my father said. "But I'll tell you how long I have. One day longer than my wife. I love her too much to leave the planet without her."

And so it was, to the amazement of everyone who didn't really know this love-matched pair, that Mom passed away at the age of 85 and Dad followed one year later when he was 86. Near the end, he told my brothers and me that those 17 years were the best six months he ever spent.

To the wonderful doctors and nurses at the Department of Veterans' Affairs Medical Center at Long Beach, he was a walking miracle. They kept a loving watch on him and just couldn't understand how a body so riddled with cancer could continue to function so well.

My dad's explanation was simple. He informed them that he had been a medic in World War I and saw amputated arms and legs, and he had noticed that none of them could think. So he decided he would tell his body how to behave. Once, as he stood up and it was evident he felt a stabbing pain, he looked down at his chest and shouted, "Shut up! We're having a party here."

Two days before he left us he said, "Boys, I'll be with your mother very soon and someday, some place we'll all be together again. But take your time about joining us; your mother and I have a lot of catching up to do."

It is said that love is stronger than prison walls. Dad proved it was a heck of a lot stronger than tiny cancer cells.

Bob, George and I are still here, armed with Dad's final gift.

A goal, a love and a dream
give you total control
over your body and your life.

The Hugging Judge

by Jack Canfield
and Mark Victor Hansen

Lee Shapiro is a retired judge. He is also one of the most genuinely loving people we know. At one point in his career, Lee realized that love is the greatest power there is. As a result, Lee became a hugger. He began offering everybody a hug. His colleagues dubbed him "the hugging judge" (as opposed to the hanging judge, we suppose). The bumper sticker on his car reads "Don't bug me! Hug me!"

About six years ago Lee created what he calls his *Hugger Kit*. On the outside it reads "A heart for a hug." The inside contains 30 little red embroidered hearts with stickums on the back. Lee will take out his Hugger Kit, go around to people and offer them a little red heart in exchange for a hug.

Lee has become so well known for this that he is often invited to keynote conferences and conventions, where he shares his message of unconditional love. At a conference in San Francisco, the local news media challenged him by saying, "It is easy to give out hugs here in the conference to people who self-selected to be here. But this would never work in the real world."

They challenged Lee to give away some hugs on the streets of San Francisco. Followed by a television crew from the local news station, Lee went out onto the street. First he approached a woman walking by. "Hi, I'm Lee Shapiro, the hugging judge. I'm giving out these hearts in exchange for a hug." "Sure," she replied. "Too easy," challenged the local commentator. Lee looked around. He saw a meter maid who was being given a hard time by the owner of a BMW to whom she was giving a ticket. He marched up to her, camera crew in tow, and said, "You look like you could use a hug. I'm the hugging judge, and I'm offering you one." She accepted.

The television commentator threw down one final challenge. "Look, here comes a bus. San Francisco bus drivers are the toughest, crabbiest, meanest people in the whole town. Let's see you get him to hug you." Lee took the challenge.

As the bus pulled up to the curb, Lee said, "Hi, I'm Lee Shapiro, the hugging judge. This has got to be one of the most stressful jobs in the whole world. I'm offering hugs to people today to lighten the load a little. Would you like one?" The six-foot-two, 230-pound bus driver got out of his seat, stepped down and said, "Why not?"

Lee hugged him, gave him a heart and waved good-bye as the bus pulled out. The TV crew was speechless. Finally, the commentator said, "I have to admit, I'm very impressed."

One day Lee's friend Nancy Johnston showed up on his doorstep. Nancy is a professional clown, and she was wearing her clown costume, makeup and all. "Lee, grab a bunch of your Hugger Kits and let's go out to the home for the disabled."

When they arrived at the home, they started giving out balloon hats, hearts and hugs to the patients. Lee was uncomfortable. He had never before hugged people who were terminally ill, severely retarded or quadriplegic. It was definitely a stretch. But after a while it became easier with Nancy and Lee acquiring an entourage of doctors, nurses and orderlies who followed them from ward to ward.

After several hours they entered the last ward. These were 34 of the worst cases Lee had seen in his life. The feeling was so grim it took his heart away. But out of their commitment to share their love and to make a difference, Nancy and Lee started working their way around the room followed by the entourage of medical staff, all of whom by now had hearts on their collars and balloon hats on their heads.

Finally, Lee came to the last person, Leonard. Leonard was wearing a big white bib which he was drooling on. Lee looked at Leonard dribbling onto his bib and said, "Let's go, Nancy. There's no way we can get through to this person." Nancy replied, "C'mon, Lee. He's a fellow human being, too, isn't he?" Then she placed a funny balloon hat on his head. Lee took one of his little red hearts and placed it on Leonard's bib. He took a deep breath, leaned down and gave Leonard a hug.

All of a sudden Leonard began to squeal, "Eeeeehh! Eeeeeehh!" Some of the other patients in the room began to clang things together. Lee turned to the staff for some sort of explanation only to find that every doctor, nurse and orderly was crying. Lee asked the head nurse, "What's going on?"

Lee will never forget what she said: "This is the first time in 23 years we've ever seen Leonard smile."

How simple it is to make a difference in the lives of others.

The Blind Man

by Helice Bridges

Buses, trains, airplanes and airports offer a safe haven for strangers to divulge intimate stories, knowing that they will probably never see one another again. Such was the case on this day in the spring of 1983 at La Guardia Airport. I was waiting for my plane when a tall, strong, handsomely tailored gentleman felt safe enough in his anonymity to sit next to me and share the following story:

"I was finishing up my work at my office in downtown Manhattan. My secretary had left about a half hour before, and I was just getting ready to pack up for the day when the phone rang. It's Ruth, my secretary. She's in a panic. 'I've left an important package on my desk by mistake. It needs to be immediately delivered to the Blind Institute. It's only a few blocks away. Could you help me out?'

"'You caught me at a good time; I was just walking out the door. Sure. I'll drop the package off for you.'

"As I walked into the Blind Institute, a man ran toward me. 'Thank heaven you arrived. We must get started at once.' He pointed to an empty chair next to him and told me to sit down. Before I could say anything, I was sitting in a row of people who were all sighted. Directly facing us was a row of sightless men and women. A young man, about 25 years old, stood in front of the room. He began giving us instructions.

"'In a moment, I will ask those of you who are sightless to get to know the person seated across from you. It will be important for you to take whatever time you need to distinguish their features, hair texture, bone type, rate of breathing and so forth. When I say "begin," you will reach across and touch the person's head, feel the texture of their hair, note if it is curly, straight, coarse or thin. Imagine what color it might be. Then slowly place your fingers on their brow. Feel the strength, the size, the texture of the skin. Use both hands to investigate the eyebrows, eyes, nose, cheekbones, lips, chin and neck. Listen to the person's breathing. Is it calm or rapid? Can you hear the heart beating? Is it fast or slow? Take your time – and now, begin.'

"I began to panic. I wanted out of this place. I don't allow anybody to touch me without my permission, let alone a man. He's touching my hair. God, this is uncomfortable. Now his hands are on my face; I'm perspiring. He'll hear my heart beating and know I'm panicking. Got to calm down, can't show him that I'm not in control. I felt a sigh of relief when it was finally over.

"'Next,' the young instructor continued, 'the sighted people will have the same opportunity to discover the person seated across from them. Close your eyes and imagine that you have never seen this person in your life. Decide what you want to know about this person. Who are they? What are their thoughts? What kind of dreams might they have? Reach across and begin to touch their head. Feel the texture of their hair. What color is their hair?'

"His voice faded in the background. Before I could stop, I had my hand on the young man's head seated across from me. His hair felt dry and coarse. I couldn't remember the color of his hair. Hell, I never remembered the color of anybody's hair.

"In fact, I'd never really looked at anyone. I just told people what to do. People were dispensable to me – I never really cared about them. My business was important, the deals I made were important. This touching, feeling and knowing other people was definitely not me, nor would it ever be.

"I continued to touch the young man's eyebrows, nose, cheeks and chin. I felt myself weeping inside. There was a tenderness in my heart that I had not known, a vulnerability I never revealed to myself or anyone else around me. I felt it and was afraid. It was clear to me that I would be out of this building very soon. I would go and never come back.

"Dreams? Did this young man across from me have dreams? Why should I care? He's nothing to me.

I've got two teenage kids – I don't even know their dreams. Besides, all they ever think of is cars, sports and girls. We don't talk much. I don't think they like me. I don't think I understand them. My wife – well, she does her thing, and I do mine.

"I'm perspiring and breathing hard. The instructor tells us to stop. I put my hand down and sit back. 'Now,' he goes on, 'this is the last part of the exercise. You will each have three minutes to share with each other the experience you had getting to know your partner. Let your partner know what you were thinking and feeling. Tell them what you learned about them. The sightless person will go first.'

"My partner's name was Henry. He told me that at first he felt left out because he didn't think he was going to have a partner for the evening. He was glad I was able to make it on time. He went on to tell me that he felt I truly had courage to take the risks to emote and feel. 'I was impressed,' he explained, 'at the way you followed the instructions despite how resistant you were to them. Your heart is very lonely and very big. You want more love in your life, but you don't know how to ask for it. I admire your willingness to discover the side of you that truly makes a difference. I know you wanted to bolt out of the room, but you stayed. I felt the same way when I first came here. But now I'm not as afraid of who I am anymore. It's okay for me to cry, feel afraid, panic, want to run, shut down from others, hide out in my work. These are just normal emotions that I am learning to accept and appreciate. You might want to spend more time down here and learn who you really are.'

"I looked across at this young sightless Henry and wept openly. I couldn't speak. There was nothing to say. I had never known a place like this in my entire life. I had never experienced this amount of unconditional love and wisdom. The only thing I remember saying to Henry was, 'Your hair is brown, and your eyes are light.' He was probably the first person in my life whose eyes I would never forget. I was the blind man; it was Henry who had the vision to see who he was.

"It was time for the meeting to end. I picked up the envelope under my seat and brought it to the instructor. 'My secretary was supposed to drop this off to you earlier this evening. Sorry it got here late.'

"The instructor smiled and took the package, saying, 'This is the first time I have ever run an evening like this. I've been waiting for the instructions to arrive so I would know what to do. When they didn't, I just had to wing it. I didn't realize you weren't one of the regular volunteers. Please accept my apologies.'

"I haven't told anyone, not even my secretary, that I go to the Blind Institute two nights each week. I can't explain it, but I actually think I'm starting to feel love for people. Don't tell anyone on Wall Street I said that. You know, it's a dog-eat-dog world, and I have to stay on top of it – or do I? I don't seem to have answers to anything anymore.

"I know I've got a lot of learning to do if my sons are going to respect me. Funny, I've never said that before. Kids are supposed to respect their parents, or at least that's what I've always been told. Maybe it goes both ways. Maybe we can learn how to respect each other. For now, I'm beginning to learn how to respect and love myself."

Simply Said

by Roberta Tremblay

Fresh flowers are such a lovely thing of beauty. Once in a while I pick a bouquet or a single perfect rose to give to a neighbor, friend or relative.

Early one morning I gathered a beautiful bouquet of sweet-smelling long-stemmed roses for myself. The roses were definitely a delight for my eyes. While I thought about how pleasing they were for me to enjoy, a calm, gentle voice outside of myself simply said, *Give them to your friend.*

I went straight into the house and arranged the roses in a vase. Then I

wrote this note as small as I could…
"For my friend." I went across the
street to my neighbor's, who is also
one of my closest friends, and I left
the bouquet at the front door.

Later that day my friend called to
thank me. She said the flowers were a
true blessing. Late the night before
she had been arguing with one of her
children. Being cruel, as teenagers can
sometimes be, her child said to her,
"You have no friends."

What a surprise when she went to
leave for work that morning and
found not just the blessings of the
bouquet of flowers, but the tiny note
which simply said *"For my friend."*

The Magic Pebbles

by John Wayne Schlatter

Why do we have to *learn* all of this dumb stuff?"

Of all the complaints and questions I have heard from my students during my years in the classroom, this was the one most frequently uttered. I would answer it by recounting the following legend.

One night a group of nomads were preparing to retire for the evening when suddenly they were surrounded by a great light. They

knew they were in the presence of a celestial being. With great anticipation, they awaited a heavenly message of great importance that they knew must be especially for them.

Finally, the voice spoke. "Gather as many pebbles as you can. Put them in your saddle bags. Travel a day's journey, and tomorrow night will find you glad, and it will find you sad."

After having departed, the nomads shared their disappointment and anger with each other. They had expected the revelation of a great universal truth that would enable them to create *wealth, health and purpose for the world. But instead they were given a menial task that made no sense to them at all. However, the memory of the brilliance of their visitor caused each one to pick up a few pebbles and deposit them in their saddle bags while voicing their displeasure.*

They traveled a day's journey, and that night while making camp, they reached into their saddle bags and discovered every pebble they had gathered had become a diamond. They were glad they had diamonds. They were sad they had not gathered more pebbles.

It was an experience I had with a student I shall call Alan, early in my teaching career, that illustrated the truth of that legend to me.

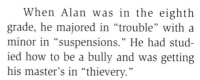

When Alan was in the eighth grade, he majored in "trouble" with a minor in "suspensions." He had studied how to be a bully and was getting his master's in "thievery."

Every day I had my students memorize a quotation from a great thinker. As I called roll, I would begin a quotation. To be counted present, the student would be expected to finish the thought.

"Alice Adams – 'There is no failure except…'"

"'In no longer trying.' I'm present, Mr. Schlatter."

So, by the end of the year, my young charges would have memorized 150 great thoughts.

"Think you can, think you can't – either way you're right!"

"If you can see the obstacles, you've taken your eyes off the goal."

"A cynic is someone who knows the price of everything and the value of nothing."

And, of course, Napoleon Hill's "If you can conceive it, and believe it, you can achieve it."

No one complained about this daily routine more than Alan – right up to the day he was expelled and I lost touch with him for five years. Then one day, he called. He was in a special program at one of the neighboring colleges and had just finished parole.

He told me that after being sent to juvenile hall and finally being shipped off to the California Youth Authority for his antics, he

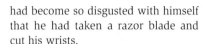

had become so disgusted with himself that he had taken a razor blade and cut his wrists.

He said, "You know what, Mr. Schlatter, as I lay there with my life running out of my body, I suddenly remembered that dumb quote you made me write 20 times one day. 'There is no failure except in no longer trying.' Then it suddenly made sense to me. As long as I was alive, I wasn't a failure, but if I allowed myself to die, I would most certainly die a failure. So with my remaining strength, I called for help and started a new life."

At the time he had heard the quotation, it was a pebble. When he needed guidance in a moment of crisis, it had become a diamond. And so it is to you I say, gather all the pebbles you can, and you can count on a future filled with diamonds.

Why Wait?...
Just Do It!

by Glenn McIntyre

My father told me that God must surely have a reason for me being the way I am today. I'm beginning to believe it.

I was the kind of kid that things always worked out for. I grew up in Laguna Beach, California, and I loved surfing and sports. But at a time when most kids my age thought only of TV and the beach, I started thinking of ways I could become more independent, see the country and plan my future.

I began working at the age of 10. By the time I was 15, I worked between one to three jobs after school. I made enough money to buy a new motorcycle. I didn't even know how to ride it. But after paying cash for the bike and one year's worth of full insurance coverage, I went to parking lots and learned to ride it. After 15 minutes of figure eights, I rode home. I was 15½, had just received my driver's permit and had bought a new motorcycle. It changed my life.

I wasn't one of those just-for-fun weekend riders. I loved to ride. Every spare minute of every day, every chance I got, I averaged 100 miles a day on top of that bike. Sunsets and sunrises looked prettier when I enjoyed them from a winding mountain road. Even now, I can close my eyes and still feel the bike naturally beneath me, so naturally that it was a more familiar feeling than walking. As I rode, the cool wind gave me a feeling of total relaxation. While I explored the open road outside, inside I was dreaming about what I wanted my life to be.

Two years and five new motorcycles later, I ran out of roads in California. I read motorcycle magazines every night, and one night, a BMW motorcycle ad caught my eye. It showed a muddy motorcycle with a duffel bag on the back parked on the side of a dirt road in front of a large "Welcome to Alaska" sign. One year later, I took a photograph of an even muddier motorcycle in front of that exact same sign. Yes, it was me! At 17 years old I made it to Alaska alone with my bike, conquering over 1,000 miles of dirt highway.

Prior to departing for my seven-week, 17,000-mile camping adventure, my friends said that I was crazy. My parents said that I should wait. Crazy? Wait? For what? Since I was a kid, I had dreamed about going across America on a motorcycle. Something strong inside of me told me that if I didn't go on this trip now, I never would. Besides, when would I have the time? I would be starting college on a scholarship very soon, then a career, perhaps even a family someday.

I didn't know if it was just to satisfy me or if in my mind I felt it would somehow transform me from a boy to a man. But what I did know was that for that summer, I was going on the adventure of a lifetime.

I quit all of my jobs, and because I was only 17, I had my mother write a letter stating that I had her permission to go on this trip. With $1,400 in my pocket, two duffel bags, a shoe box full of maps strapped to the back of my motorcycle, a pen flashlight for protection and a lot of enthusiasm, I left for Alaska and the East Coast.

I met a lot of people, enjoyed the rugged beauty and lifestyle, ate off the open fire and thanked God every day for giving me this opportunity. Sometimes, I didn't see or hear anyone for two or three days and just rode my motorcycle in endless silence with only the wind racing around my helmet. I didn't cut my hair, I took cold showers at campgrounds when I could, and I even had several unscheduled confrontations with bears during that trip. It was the greatest adventure!

Even though I took several more trips, none can ever compare to that summer. It has always held a special place in my life. I can never go back again and explore the roads and mountains, the forests and glacial waters the same way I did back then on that trip, alone with my motorcycle. I can never make the same trip in the exact same way because at the age of 23, I was in a motorcycle accident on a street in Laguna Beach where I was hit by a drunk driver/drug dealer who left me paralyzed from the ribs down.

At the time of my accident, I was in great shape, both physically and mentally. I was a full-time police officer, still riding my motorcycle on my days off. I was married and financially secure. I had it made. But in the space of less than a second, my whole life changed. I spent eight months in the hospital, got divorced, saw that I could not return to work in the way that I had known it, and, along with learning how to deal with chronic pain and a wheelchair, I saw all the dreams I had for my future leaving my reach. Luckily for me, help and support helped new dreams to develop and be fulfilled.

When I think back to all of those trips I took, all of those roads that I traveled, I think of how lucky I was to have been able to do that. Every time I rode, I always said to myself, "Do it now. Enjoy your surroundings, even if you're at a smoggy city intersection; enjoy life because you cannot depend on getting a second chance to be in the same place or do the same things."

After my accident, my father said that God had a reason for me being a paraplegic. I believe it. It has made me a stronger person. I returned to work as a desk officer, bought a home and married again. I also have my own consulting business and am a professional speaker. Every now and again, when things get rough, I remind myself of all the things that I have accomplished, all the things I have yet to accomplish and my father's words.

Yes, he was right. God sure did have a reason. Most importantly, I remind myself to enjoy every moment of every day. And if you can do something, do it. Do it now!